Another Dam Picture Book

Photos of Rogue River Dams:
Gold Ray Dam
Gold Hill Dam
Savage Rapids Dam
Golden Drift Dam
Ament Dam
Grants Pass Dam

Photos compiled and comments written by
Joan Momsen

Design and layout by Joan Momsen
Copyright 2009, Josephine County Historical Society
Second Printing c. 2017, Josephine County Historical Society
All rights reserved
ISBN-13:978-1544031880
ISBN-10:1544031882

Digital photography has changed the way we view, take and save photographs. Because we do not use film, we do not print all photos, only special ones. Without the cost of film people can snap, snap, and snap photos at a rapid rate. Printing them all would get expensive. One views them immediately and discards ones that they do not like. The long process of loading the camera, checking the light, taking photos few and far between is long gone. You don't have to think of the cost and the limited length of the roll of film. You buy your chip that holds 500 or so photos and snap anything and everything. You download it to your computer, save the ones you want on compact discs, and view them all on your computer, or convert the CD's to DVD's and watch them on your television. Photo albums have given way to computer presentations. Those who remember sitting and watching slide presentations, now have to stand behind the host as she maneuvers the computer to show the latest snapshots. Is this progress? Slide shows are what they are still called but not a single 35mm slide exists. You no longer sit and watch the big screen while slide after slide is projected on the screen or wall. You watch a small computer screen or a larger flat screen television.

I am guilty of the above. However, I still believe hat nothing beats a well-framed black and white photograph. Even a poorly framed black and white photo has a story to tell. In this book, for most of the photos, I have not cropped or changed the original photo. I scanned it as it was and you see what the original looked like, flaws and all.

Some have comments on them, some are from old publications, some are fuzzy, crooked and not very clear, but that is what I was able to find. We do not know what our descendants will be looking at 100 years from now, but I would venture to guess that the 200 year-old black and white photo will survive better than the 100 year-old digital DC.

So take out your magnifying glass and look at the details of the old photos. Even the 2009 black and white digital photos have something to reveal. This is a picture book. Do not flip rapidly through the pages. Study the photos. Enjoy the process.

When you finish the photographic portion of the book, there are brief comments about the dams at the end. There probably is much more to be written about the topic, however, this venture was started as *Another Dam Picture Book* not a written commentary, but I had to tell the basic story of the history of the dams. I did this by reading what we had at the Josephine County Historical Society and choosing what briefly told the story. Most articles had to be retyped because the originals were on microfilm. Some short articles of interest were photocopied and credit given if it was available.

And, as I like to say with most things I publish, if you have historical information that might enlighten future researchers, we would like to have copies at the Josephine County Historical Society. We will scan your original photos while you wait. We will start a file on your family if you give us your story. Join us in keeping the history of Josephine County in a safe place for future generations to research.

Joan Momsen

Index

Gold Ray Dam

Gold Ray Dam will be the last dam of the five dams shown in this book to be removed. This was a photo taken around 1905 when the dam (to the right) and the power house (across the river behind the group of people) were new. We will proceed downriver to Grants Pass with most of the photos about the three dams (Savage Rapids, Ament and the Grants Pass Diversion Dam) in Josephine County. Gold Ray and Gold Hill Diversion Dams are in Jackson County.

In the spring of 2009, the Gold Ray Dam's deserted power house stands silently on the north side of the Rogue River. Photo was taken May 17, 2009.

Gold Ray Dam, May 17, 2009, Photos of Gold Ray Dam taken
by Joan Momsen

Gold Ray Dam with railroad tracks in the foreground, fish ladder at center on north side of the river with the power house to the left. Photo taken May 17, 2009

The original Gold Ray Dam was a wooden structure. An early newspaper article refers to it as the Condor Dam. Evidently, the name was changed to name it after the Ray brothers who built the first dam. Photo taken May 17, 2009.

The concrete version of the Gold Ray Dam with the fish ladder, was built in the 1940s. Gold Ray provided power to the Rogue Valley for over 70 years. Photo taken May 17, 2009.

Gold Hill Dam

The Gold Hill Diversion Dam was 900 feet long and 8 feet high. It diverted water for the use of the Ideal Cement Company and provided drinking water for city of Gold Hill. After Gold Hill built a pumping station, the dam was removed. This photo was taken May 17, 2008

Photo Courtesy of WaterWatch, photo by Bob Hunter.

This is what the site of the Gold Hill dam looked like on July 28, 2008 after the dam was removed. Of the five dams pictured in this book, the Gold Hill Dam was the youngest and the third to be removed. Savage Rapids and Gold Ray are next.

The old deserted Gold Hill power plant sits silently on the north bank of the Rogue River near the site of the removed dam. Picture taken May 17, 2009 by Joan Momsen.

Savage Rapids Dam

Fishing at Savage Rapids c. 1915 BD   (Before Dam).

This is a view of Savage Rapids before the dam. Savage
Rapids was named for the Savage family who homesteaded
just upstream from the rapids.

After they got started on the dam construction and had
the bridge built across the river at the site of the
proposed Savage Rapids Dam, the rains came and the
river rose.

As seen from above, the temporary bridge across the
Rogue River was almost covered by the rapid rising flood
waters. Most of the rocks, as seen in the previous photo,
were under water. The equipment and supplies under
the bridge were also under water or swept away.
However, the men standing on the bridge evidently
thought it was strong enough to withstand the rushing
water.

Upstream from the scaffolding, the construction shacks
and supplies were washed here and there, but it looks
like most did not get past the scaffold bridge.

The Grants Pass Irrigation District sent out a small album of selected construction photos to some community members as a Christmas card/gift in 1921. Some of these photos were not included and therefore not dated.

After the water went down, they had quite a jumble to straighten out.

People came to the site to see what had happened.

Soon the steam shovels were fired up and the
construction of Savage Rapids Dam began again.

The construction crews were probably glad they did not have a long drive home or to a hotel. The barracks probably looked good to them after a long day of working in the muck.

No details were written on the photos, so one can assume besides barracks for the men, they probably had an office , maybe a separate shower facility and a cookhouse to prepare the meals.

This photo shows the rails across the bridge. The round "things" in the forefront are the giant buckets with rail wheels. They were filled with the concrete mixed at the plant shown on the next page and wheeled out over the specific panel of the dam that was being poured that day. Other views of the concrete facility can be seen in other photos on the south side of the river. They not only built a dam, they built a series of rail tracks that can be seen in various positions at the dam site.

A sawmill was built on the site to provide all the wood needed for the construction project.

Trees were cut on site and were milled and cut to specifications for the dam construction.

Panels 1 to 5 were completed in 1920. This photo was taken July 9, 1921 shortly after the resumption of work on the dam in 1921. A secondary cofferdam was constructed to catch leakage from the main cofferdam.

The building of the dam moved quickly. This photo shows the preparation of the raft for the final closure of the cofferdam in front of panels 6 to 9 on July 19, 1921.

In this photo the crew is closing the secondary cofferdam to stop leakage on July 22, 1921. The size of the project can be judged by looking at the men on the site. This is where that magnifying glass could be really useful.

This shows the lower cofferdam by panels 6 and 7. The crew is cleaning out gravel along the toe of the dam to permit the water to tail-race. Forms for panels 8 and 9 were being erected in this July 27, 1921 photo.

On August 23, 1921 panels 13 and 14 on the extreme left are completed. Panels 6-7-8-9 to the right of the diversion channel are ready to pour.

On Sept 10, 1921 the dam was complete except for the portion at the diversion channel. The main cofferdam was taken out by drag line buckets preparatory to diverting the river flow through sluice-gates underneath the power house.

This is the last photo of water in the by-pass. The dark fringe along the rocks at the right of the flow of the river shows the river level had lowered two feet by part of the flow being diverted though the sluice-gates. Taken about 3 PM on September 10, 1921, this shows the dam completed except for the panels (10-11-12) to be built across the by-pass.

On September 14, 1921 this photo shows the cofferdam across the by-pass channel being closed. The river was flowing through the sluice-gates under the power house.

By September 20, 1921 panels 10, 11 and 12 at the former by-pass channels were completed to within six feet of the crest of the dam and the rest of the forms were ready for pouring the concrete to the crest level.

By September 28, 1921 the last three panels (10, 11, 12) were completed to the crest of the dam and the segmental gate hinges and gates at the crest of the dam were being installed.

This view with too much light to the left of the print, was not part of the Christmas card, but it shows a good ground level view of the completed spillways.

This is the powerhouse flume with the turbine and hydraucone chambers shown at the bottom. I-beams to support the trash rack are shown in the front. Barely visible to the right is the fishway. Photo taken October 7, 1921.

View of the finished dam as seen from the south side of the river. Photo was taken from old Highway 99 on November 4, 1921, the day before the official dedication of the dam.

The lake is full with water flowing two feet deep over the crest of the dam. The newly erected footbridge across the dam is clearly visible in this photo taken November 4, 1921. The next day the dam was dedicated. Photos of the dedication of the dam will follow the remaining views of the dam taken after the official "opening" of the dam.

Curtain gates controlling in-flow water supply to the turbines are down (closed) in this view. The sluice-gates are open and the river is flowing underneath the dam. Photo taken November 12, 1921

This upstream view of the multiple arch type hollow concrete
dam was taken November 12. 1921. The dam was hollow with a
tunnel inside.   Over the years, as the dam was strengthened
and remodeled, this view disappeared under a layer of concrete.

On November 15, 1922 the steel suspension bridge spanning the 240 foot wide Rogue River is shown with the double line 24 inch steel pipe which supplied irrigation water to the North End Unit.

This photo of the dry fish ladder was not one of the photos that was part of the Christmas card, but it is taken from a different angle than the one that follows.

The north side fish ladder allowed the fish to swim over the dam. The top of the ladder was on the north side of the power plant. Photo was taken November 17, 1921.

Taken November 17, 1921, this shows the flow of the river being retained above the dam by the closed sluice-gates. The fish ladder continued to flow. It is just visible in the lower left corner of the photo. The river was flowing under the power house.

Although not noted in the written material we have looked at, November 17, 1921 obviously was a date to test the sluice-gates and the flow of the water under and over the dam. This shows 1900 second feet flowing over the crest of the dam.

This and the previous two photos show a good view of the footbridge over the dam. This photo taken on November 30, 1921 shows the water flowing over the dam at a depth of 7.1 feet at the crest.

On December 23, 1921 this photo shows the water flowing with a depth of 9 feet on the crest of the dam with a Tainter gate in a lowered position.

On July 14, 1922 this general view of the dam shows what it looked liked during irrigation season. In the foreground is the out-let box showing the water being discharged into the South Highland canal.

Taken July 29, 1922 the photo shows the picture postcard view of the dam. This photo was reproduced many times on postcards. The canal intake is at the extreme right, the power house is on the other side of the river at the end of the dam and the 42 inch pipe line supplying the Tokay Canal in the background. The Southern Pacific Railroad main line track is on the opposite side of the Rogue River.

Regressing to November 5, 1921, this is the official view of the
dedication ceremonies for Savage Rapids Dam. This photo was
included with the preceding construction photos in the photo
album/Christmas card that was sent to dam patrons in 1921.
The crowd, estimated at 3,000 people, came to view the newly
completed Savage Rapids Dam at the November 1921
dedication ceremony.

People were allowed to wander over the site or cross over the dam on the footbridge. Shortly after the dam went into operation, the footbridge was washed away by flood waters. Notice there is no fish ladder on the south side of the river.

This and the following photo were taken when the dam was new, but obviously by a photographer with a different camera. The flags strung across the river above the dam show up better in this photograph than the official photos.

Look at the small distance between the crest of the dam and the
footbridge. One wonders what the builders were thinking
about because in a short time, high flood waters washed the
bridge away.

After a snowfall, this man braved the danger of the slippery rocks at Savage Rapids to have his photo taken with the rushing water.

Photo courtesy of the Grants Pass

Irrigation District.

This observation tower was built on the north side of the river many years after the dedication of the dam. In the center are the two curtain gates used to restrict the flow into the turbines. This photo was taken in the 1950s.

Taken in 1950s, the curtain gates are open. The curtain gates are the rolls to the left in this picture.

Photo courtesy of the Grants Pass Irrigation District

This stepped bulkhead was constructed in the 1950s.

Savage Rapids Dam had extensive reconstruction in the 1950s. This is a photo of the "new" dam.

View of the remodeled dam taken from the north side of the Rogue River.

P712-100-114 Savage Rapids Dam Rehabilitation; aerial view taken by Airphoto Service of America. Grants Pass Project, OR. CNST/General. BR photo copy by R.A. Baker, July 18, 1953.

Photo courtesy of the Grants Pass Irrigation District

Taken in 1953, this view of the dam shows the cofferdam holding back the water as modification was completed on the dam.

This view of the dam shows the safety line of barrels in the lake giving warning to boaters to turn around and not go over the dam. Also the gates shown in the following photo have been installed.

Taken in the 1970s this photo shows the preparation of one of the gates to be lifted into place. The arches of the original dam panels have been covered (reinforced) with concrete.

In the 1970s the upstream side of the dam looked as it often did as the irrigation district dredged the accumulated sand out from behind the dam before the gates were placed for the summer irrigation season.

The rocks behind the dam show why boaters needed to be cautious until the lake was full. Once the lake was filled, a safety line was put across the river so boaters would not inadvertently steer their boats over the dam.

In the 1980s the dam was showing its age as various groups
discussed another rejuvenation or removal. Removal won.

Before the removal of the dam began, the pumping station had
to be built. This photo shows the site of the area where the
building was constructed. This gives a good view of the dam.
The powerhouse and fish ladder on the north side and part of
the spillway structure on the south side will remain. This
photo was taken c. 2007.

In 2009 the removal of the dam began. This picture shows the beginning of the cofferdam on the north side of the river. Sand and gravel was dumped in front of the dam and then upon that base, the cofferdam was built. Photo taken April 13, 2009

The workers are putting down a waterproof tarp which was then covered with sand within the plywood cribbing and pulled upward where another tarp and another layer of sand applied. This was done on both sides of the cofferdam. Notice the large tree trunk with roots resting on the dam. Photo taken April 13, 2009. Unless otherwise stated, the following photos of the removal of Savage Rapids dam were taken by Joan Momsen.

The bridge to the left carries the pipe across the river. It is used to put water in the canal north of the river. Photo taken April 13, 2009.

In the upper right of this photo, the roadway down to the gravel bar on the north side of the river can be seen. Backhoes dug the sand and gravel from the river bed upstream. The sand and grave accumulated on the lakebed provided material to build the cofferdam. The sand/gravel loads were hauled by trucks that backed down to the cofferdam and emptied their loads. A truck and backhoe can be seen just upstream behind the dam.

Photo taken April 13, 2009.

The shore line, which when the dam was filled was the lake bed, on the north side of the river provided the sand and gravel for the cofferdam. The road can be seen where the trucks went upstream to get the sand and gravel.

The tree trunk with roots is still resting on the dam. The layers of the cofferdam are to the left in this photo. Photo taken April 21, 2009 at 4:52 PM.

A backhoe and roller are shown leveling out the top of the cofferdam just before quitting time on April 21, 2009.

This shows the two parallel rows of steel pilings on the upstream side of the dam. The space between the pilings was filled with sand and gravel to form the cofferdam and also provide the roadbed to add sand and gravel to the down steam side of the cofferdam after it was built to the top of the dam.

The flow of the water is very low at the upstream side of the
dam. Notice the cofferdam in the background to compare as the
water rises. Photo taken April 21, 2009.

On April 27, 2009 the sandbar, where the sand and gravel was dug for the cofferdam, has disappeared under the rising water and has again become the lakebed.

Three men stand on the observation platform looking at the completed cofferdam as water flows through the south side fish ladder.

On May 2, 2009 the cofferdam on the downsteam side
of the dam shows the multi-layer construction as water
on the nearest spillway laps up against the bottom edge.

The up steam portion of the cofferdam has the rising water lapping against the bottom as the water trapped behind it was being pumped out. A plastic fence and plywood "guard rail" was placed along the edge of the cofferdam. Photo taken about 2 PM May 2, 2009.

The covers to the water intake pipes sit in a row below the bridge and pumping facility.

It started to rain the evening before and by 3 PM on May 4, 2009, part of the cofferdam had been washed out. Large white sandbags were placed at the top of the spillway next to the cofferdam, and in this photo the backhoe is dropping more sandbags by the washed out area.

The unexpected downpour raised the river and began to wash out the sand, causing the tarp to hang limply over the side of the cofferdam. The backhoe is shown dropping the large white sacks of sand below the spillway to prevent further erosion.

On May 5, 2009 the Komatsu backhoe moved sand and gravel into the washed out area. The white sandbags at the base of the washout are under water.

A couple of days later the water level had lowered but the plastic safety fence hung limply over the washout as more sand was washed away.

The cofferdam was not rebuilt, but sand, gravel and rocks were dropped in the gap to prevent further erosion. The demolition company said they could start to remove the dam without rebuilding the cofferdam.

Upstream there was not much water damage because the steel pilings pounded into the riverbed could not be washed away as easily as the sand.   This photo was taken May 11, 2009.

The site sat idle while decisions were made.

The river remained high but the rain was only a weekend event.
This photo was taken May 11.

The section of the dam slated for removal can be seen to the left of this photo which looks at the dam through the substation and parking lot for the pumping facility. Photo taken May 11.

Some progress was made where the washed out portion of the
cofferdam was backfilled and the bright orange plastic fence
was pulled away from the washout. Photo taken
May 13, 2009.

The dam sat awaiting the beginning of removal of the north side in June.

Things remained almost untouched for about three weeks.

May 29th showed very little difference at the dam site. The backhoes with special dam busting attachments were moved closer to the dam.

The last view of the intact north side of the dam is clearly shown. Also the metal pilings driven into the riverbed on the backside of the dam stand guard over the soon to be removed portion of the dam. This photo was taken May 29, 2009.

Most of the construction clutter has been cleared from the pump
building parking lot.

101Photo courtesy of WaterWatch, Photo taken by Bob Hunter.

June 1, 2009 removal of the dam begins as a backhoe with a ram punches holes in panels 2 and 3. This was not a difficult job because the dam was hollow with a tunnel inside. This and the other WaterWatch photos can be seen on the WaterWatch website.

After the edges were punched, the center part was removed by "following the dotted line." This photo also taken on June 1, 2009 by Bob Hunter for WaterWatch.

With the concrete removed, the dark tunnel can be seen. There was no turning back. Savage Rapids Dam will be history by December 2009. After the panel was removed, the opening was used as a gateway as the heavy equipment moved to the backside of the dam and carried out all the debris before continuing on the front side.

Photo courtesy of the Grants Pass Daily Courier, Jeff Duewel, photographer

June 9th, 2000: this photo was published in the *Grants Pass Daily Courier.* Jeff Duewel was the photographer. "A hoe ram, left, and hydraulic shear, right are being used to tear out the north side of Savage Rapids Dam this week." The magnifying glass has been provided for you to look closer at this picture on the next two pages.

F.

Photo courtesy of the Grants Pass Daily Courier, Jeff Duewel, photographer.

Photo courtesy of the Grants Pass Daily Courier, Jeff Duewel, photographer

By June 9, 2009 the north side of the dam was quickly being removed. Backhoes worked on both sides of the dam.

June 10, 2009 this photo was published in the *Grants Pass Daily Courier*. Kevin Launius was the photographer. "A hydraulic shear chews away concrete at Savage Rapids Tuesday afternoon." On the following page there is a magnified view. Savage Rapids Dam was hollow with a tunnel running through it. This and the next photo show why it was relatively easy to knock down.

Photo courtesy of the Grants Pass Daily Courier, Keven Launius , photographer

The dam project after the north side of dam was removed.

June 20, 2009 most of the debris of the demolished dam has been removed.

Here is a view of the pumping station and the bridge with the pipe carrying water across the river to the highline ditch.

A few days later, the north end of the dam and much of the sand behind it has been removed. The tarp has also been flattened and covered with sand. The excess sand has been pushed over the edge, probably as a bunker against another heavy rainfall. Water is starting to accumulate under the old fish ladder.

On July 23, 2009 three backhoes work to pull out the sand and gravel of the cofferdam behind the removed portion of the dam.

115

This and the previous photo show the inside of the cofferdam and even though part of it washed away in the high water, enough remained for the north side of the dam to be quickly and thoroughly removed.

By August 3 the pool of water has reached the bottom of the old fish ladder, but all else looks much like it will look until October when the south side spillways will be removed.

August 3 there is a man on the roof of the pumping station. When the dam is gone, Grants Pass Irrigation District will have this structure to manage instead of the old dam.

This is probably what it will look like until the next stage of deconstruction begins.

The man is still on the roof, some of the covers to the intake pipes are all neatly lined up below the pumping facility and the river continues to flow.

With almost three weeks of 100+ degrees of temperature, the flow of the Rogue River did not slow down and the seepage into the low area behind the cofferdam continued to raise the water level.

Part of the remaining south side panels of the dam will not be removed and will act as a buffer to deflect flood waters away from the pumping station.

On August 30, 2009, a lone fish, no doubt a salmon, jumps up the spillway, ignoring the fish ladder in the foreground. After 88 years, she is one of last to make the up steam jump over Savage Rapids Dam.

Golden Drift Dam
also know as
Ament Dam

Oxen were used to move heavy items at the site of Golden
Drift Dam. A camp was built so construction crews could live
on the site.

Taken March 2, 1902, this shot shows the cribs constructed of 12 by 12 timbers with crushed rocks placed in some of the cribs. This view is looking downstream at the north bank of the Rogue River.

A damaged negative produced this view of the same construction shown in the previous picture and the three that follow.

Again another view of the north side crib construction. Notice the tall pole in the photo and note its location in the two following photos taken at different angles.

This view looked toward the south side of the river, where the bank was considerably higher. It shows the same north side portion of the dam. This view was looking upstream.

In this photo taken from the south side of the river, the same dam construction also shows the right-of-way of the Southern Pacific Railroad in the background.

This and the follow photo are two bent and warped pictures of the backside of the wing dam obviously taken at about the same time as the rope (cable) in the foreground is in the same general area is both photos.

Here a worker walks through the mud behind the dam (upstream side).

This photo was taken on the downstream side of the dam, just below the site shown in the previous two photos. This was photographed after all the crushed rocks were in the cribs and water was flowing over the dam across the river and the wing dam along the north side. The water is flowing through the gates of the wing dam section.

With snow on the mountains, the water is flowing over the Golden Drift Dam at what looks like high water or low flood stage.

The Josephine County Irrigation and Placer Company's dam, showing the "intake"

Taken from a 1909 Commercial Club publication, this "foldout" shows a good view of the width of the dam. Notice all the people standing above the dam's gates.

of the great irrigation system under construction at Grants Pass

The south side fish ladder is shown at the far right.

Many photos were taken of the low Golden Drift Dam, but there are only a few of the higher Ament Dam.

Golden Drift Dam, Grants Pass, Ore.

This picture of the Golden Drift Dam was also used as a postcard. The following picture is the same but with a handwritten comment in 1906. The wing dam portion to the left of this photo was wood with rocks and some concrete and the main dam across the river was wood cribs filled with crushed rocks.

GOLDEN DRIFT MINING COMPANY'S DAM, GRANTS PASS, OREGON

The "X" marks the spot if one wants to go looking for a gold mine. Things have probably changed in the hills since Jan 22, 1906.

About 300 people attended the ceremonies of the opening of the irrigation canal at the Golden Drift Dam. Many of them rode the train out to the dam site.

Grants Pass Mayor H.C. Kinney, with shovel in hand, stands in
The foreground of the canal-opening ceremony on June 10,
1909.

This was a good site and opportunity for a photo but not the safest way to do so.

*An immense centrifugal pump used by the Irrigation and Power Company
of Josephine County at Grants Pass*

The size of the pump can readily be seen because of the man
standing next to it. This photo was taken from a 1909
Commercial Club publication.   A newspaper article said this
was the pump that was swept away in a flood and never
recovered.

This was the type of "giant" the pump supplied with water. The giant nozzle was used to "blast" the gold laden soil at Dry Diggings. The waterfall was probably the Bloody Run Creek which flowed through Dry Diggings into the Rogue River.

Gold Drift Dam on Rogue River, Grants Pass, Ore.

This was originally a color photo of the dam taken in 1909.

At G. D. M. Co's Dam, Sunday, Aug. 14th, 1910.

In the center of this photo, the "waterfall" was the route fish had to swim to get above the dam. Maybe it was called a fish ladder, but there were no steps. Following are three more views of the same area. Notice the men along the rocky bank. This was probably a good "fishing hole" since the fish had to gather there before making the attempt to go upstream. The cribbing still surrounds the concrete powerhouse.

Look carefully at this photo and you can see the long
structure on the upstream side of the dam. It was the
wing dam that directed the water toward the pump
house. Water was funneled into the lines that went into
Grants Pass. The lines were gravity fed because the
pumps were not initially installed. However, the
following photo has a small pump with attached pipes.

149

This and the previous photo shows what passed for a fish ladder. In both photos a salmon can be seen above the flow of the water, heading upstream. This may have been a composite photo just to prove that fish could go up the ladder. Both photos are of the ladder on the north side of the river. The water flowed around and through the power plant.

A member of the Grants Pass High School Class of 1946 donated this and the next two photos to the Josephine County Historical Society in the spring of 2009. These are photos of students practicing for a play at the old Ament Dam powerhouse, which half-buried, looked much like a Medieval castle.

One of the large rectangular openings facing toward the river
provided a perfect place for a little practice swordplay in 1946,
but more importantly gives us a glimpse of how the river has
been slowly burying the remains of the dam.

This view is the same as the two photos that follow. From 1946, when this was taken, to c.1960 when the next photo was taken, the river deposited several feet of sand around the lower level of the powerhouse building.   A good guess would be the 1955 flood changed the 1946 view to the one in the 1960s.

By the 1960s the river had deposited more sand around the base of the west side. The rectangular openings facing the river still had part of the lower level of the building exposed. Since this photo was taken, the silt has built up around the entire structure. Another good guess would be that the 1964 flood deposited the sand.

The sand in the forefront covers a large outcropping of river rocks which can be seen in the previous photos of Ament Dam. A concrete slab, as a place for a picnic table, (far left) sits on the sand with the rocks buried below.

On the side facing away from the river (north side) the year
1911 tells us when this gigantic structure was built. This photo
and all the photos shown of the current status of the remains of
Ament Dam were taken May 12, 2009 by Joan Momsen.

Looking southwest, the riverbed is just below the trees. This structure was built 200 feet from the river in 1911. A portion of the dam, at a 90 degree angle from the dam that crossed the river, funneled water into the power plant.
From above, the dam looked like a giant cross.

In 1911 this was the pride of Grants Pass. The Golden Drift Mining Company's dam had become the property of the local water and power company and was used to provide water to the city. A pipeline into Grants Pass (three miles downriver) was built. The part of the structure to the left in this photo was probably the aqueduct to carry the pipeline to the vicinity of the railroad tracks and then along Ament Dam Road into the city.

Looking out toward the riverbed, these rectangular portals connected with the wooden portion of the dam. None of the pictures of the dam show these openings because the wooden structure of the dam blocks a view of them.

This shows the powerhouse and the long aqueduct stretched out toward the railroad tracks. This is the top story. The foundation and first story are buried in the sand.

Local artists have made the old building more colorful than it was in its heyday. Too bad the artists don't know the history of this grand old skeleton of a building.

Look at the photos of the dam and powerhouse when it was in its prime, and then picture yourself standing at this arch, looking down as the fish came up the fish ladder to the left and swam through the openings in the aqueduct to the waters behind the dam.

Imagine a homeward bound salmon having to swim up the waterfall called a fish ladder, climbing 200 feet above the original riverbed, swimming through these holes in the aqueduct, just to make it to the spawning grounds. Since no plans or specifications for Ament Dam were located, by looking at the old photos, one can make the assumption of how it worked.

This is where the lake behind the dam was located.   This view is looking down toward the river which would be about 300 feet from where this photo was taken.

This is the same aqueduct as the previous photo, but this is looking north toward the railroad tracks.

As you walk away from the remains of the Ament Dam located at the upstream end of Tom Pearce Park, consider the possibility of another high flood washing away the sand and once again exposing the bottom two-thirds of this building.

The Grants Pass Dam

The Rogue River looks much like this today as you look downstream from the Caveman Bridge.   However, in 1900 that "bump" in the river was the Grants Pass Diversion Dam and boats could not go over it. To the right of the dam, where the water w a s channeled to the powerhouse, you can see a wooden structure that resembles a power line.

This and the previous photo are looking downriver at the backside of the Grants Pass Power Dam. It was known as the Grants Pass Dam, The Grants Pass Diversion Dam, or The Grants Pass Power Dam. The debris in the trees indicate recent high water just before this photo was taken.

One could skim a boat over the Grants Pass Dam when the water was as high as shown in this photo, but it might capsize as it went over the spillway. This is the Grants Pass Dam as seen from the South Side of the Rogue River.   The end of 5th Street is located on the opposite side.

Dam below Rogue River Bridge 1900

As you can see in this photo, boats did not easily go below the dam. There was a marina where people could rent a variety of boats. Pictured in the background is the second bridge across the river at Grants Pass. The first one washed out in 1890.

The inscription on the photo dates it as being taken in 1900. There was a nice lake formed by the dam, and boating was a popular pastime.

Obviously the dam was a popular fishing site. The dam was angled diagonally across the river so the water could be diverted to the powerhouse and irrigation canals.

If you look to the right as you go under Caveman Bridge today, you can see remnants left over from the dam.

Old Dam and Rogue River Bridge, Grants Pass, Ore.

This postcard refers to the dam as the "old dam." Have you ever wondered why 6th Street is straight until you drive onto Caveman Bridge? When the first two bridges were built, 6th Street went straight across the river. When the third bridge was built, it was built upstream next to the old bridge, which was then removed. Finally, when Caveman Bridge was constructed, it was upstream next to the third bridge, which was then removed. You can look down stream from Caveman Bridge and see the remains of the support pillars of two previous bridges.

This view of the lake created by the Grants Pass Dam was from the bridge looking east. The bridge was downriver just a few feet from the present Caveman Bridge. If you look over the side of Caveman Bridge, you can see the remains of the support pilings from the bridges shown in the next photos. This photo shows a much larger area of water than exists in 2009. The city park is located to the right in this photo.

This photo shows a gap in the dam and you can see how far the
water has receded along the shoreline.   The trees indicate it
was wintertime. There is no comment on the photo. Maybe one
of the many floods washed out a portion of the dam. You can
See the stacked wooden timbers that made the base of the dam.
This view is looking downstream.

Taken from the south side of the river, looking upstream (east), this gives a good view of how the dam was built diagonally across the river to act as a funnel to get the water to the powerhouse (far left, out of sight). At the time of this photo, it was claimed that the bridge was the longest single span bridge in the world.

ROGUE RIVER BRIDGE, GRANTS PASS, ORE.

This is a photo of an artist-enhanced postcard. Notice the horses and wagon on the bridge. This photo was "doctored" to make a colored postcard. The artist also drew a center pillar, which did not exist. The following photo is the same scene, but untouched.

GRANTS PASS DAM 1909

This photo is untouched, unlike the previous post card. The same horses and wagon are in the same positions, but not the center support pillar. The item centered under the bridge is probably a sailboat. Trees can be seen above it. It is the same photo that has not been artist-enhanced or colored.

This photo has much to see. The dam is in the background past the bridge. To the right of the dam is the diversion channel to the powerhouse. The building must be the powerhouse and the tall pole behind it is probably the power pole that is the point of distribution for electricity for Grants Pass. In the middle are gill net stands and a sailboat is on the river. The ladies and children are posing by a boat.

This is an enlarged portion of the previous photo. The buildings seen under the bridge deck to the left must be the powerhouse complex if such a name existed. After 1905 most of the power generated for the area came from Gold Ray Dam.

Inside city limits, Grants Pass

1909

These young ladies are ready to float on the city lake in 1909. The boat is named the *John C.*

182

This is an original photograph, glued to a heavy piece of black paper. Taken from the bridge, it looks downstream at the Grants Pass Diversion Dam. As you can, see the dam goes diagonally across the river from southeast to northwest and the water is funneled into the powerhouse on the right.

This photograph is taken from the bridge and is looking up
river.   The current location of Riverside Park is to the right of
the sailboat.

Rogue River and Bridge, Grant's Pass, Ore. WILBUR   Howard
1907

The Grants Pass Dam can be seen in the background as Wilbur and Howard enjoy the lake with their boatmates in 1907. Notice the nice beach at Riverside Park. There is no explanation on the back of the photo.

Here a pleasure craft was taking advantage of the water backed upriver by the dam. The boat was moving upstream away from the dam. Notice the two boys standing on the board at the left edge of the photo. Also notice the new bridge. This bridge was replaced c.1908. The bridge seen here was in place until 1931 when Caveman Bridge replaced it. It was moved downstream to become Robertson Bridge and still stands, with the wooden deck removed, next to the new Robertson Bridge.

Undated, this photograph was taken at Riverside Park along the south shore of the Rogue River. Swimsuit styles indicate it was taken in the late 1920s or early 1930s.

The Rogue River at Riverside Park in Grants Pass was extensively used for swimming until the polio scare in the late 1940s. After that, people were cautious about where and when they went swimming in the river. There was a dock, a water slide and a raft anchored in the center of the river. The dam still held back enough water to make a good swimming area.

This photo was taken on the north side of the river looking across at the bathhouse. The underneath area housed the changing rooms and the upper level was used as a bandstand. The wooden boardwalk from the dock to the bathhouse allowed swimmers to exit the water and get to the bathhouse without walking in sand. The slide and raft were used throughout the summer because the Grants Pass Dam provided a shallow lake, unlike the low level of water in recent years.

Taken August 29, 2009 from Caveman Bridge, this photo shows the main channel of the Rogue River to the left and the dry channel to the right where the Grants Pass Diversion Dam funneled the water to the waterwheel and powerhouse.

This is the 2009 view looking east from Caveman Bridge. Recreation, irrigation and drinking water are the prime uses for the water of the Rogue River.

And now we come to the end of *Another Dam Picture Book*. This book was put together for those who think "a picture is worth a thousand words" or those who only have time to look at the pictures. The dams were built when life was slower and all outlived their usefulness.   No more power generates from Gold Ray Dam and it will be the last to be removed.   Gold Hill Diversion Dam departed in 2008 after the city of Gold Hill built a new pumping station for the river water.   Savage Rapids Dam was removed in 2009. A small portion of it will remain standing to remind us of what used to be, just as a portion of Ament Dam has sat overlooking the Rogue River for 100 years. Hundreds of people play disk golf and pass through the ruins of Ament Dam at Pearce Park and do not even have a clue as to the story behind that graffiti covered cement edifice.

And finally, the Grants Pass Dam, which held back recreational waters for over half a century, is nothing but a bump in the river as the jet boats skim over its remains. When someone said, "Dam it" over 115 years ago, he also probably never had a clue what pleasure or pain the five dams would cause the citizens of Jackson and Josephine Counties.

Another Dam Picture Book

by
Joan Momsen

This is a book of pictures of dams along the Rogue River from Gold Ray and Gold Hill Dams in Jackson County to Savage Rapids, Ament and the Grants Pass Dams in Josephine County.   When these dams were built, some over 100 years ago, they were constructed for a need that no long exists because modern technology has changed the way to get water out of the river and onto the land for irrigation, and drinking water.   The need for water-generated power has lessened at the local level too.   What may have seemed like a lot of power being generated to light the homes at the beginning of the 20th Century, is now just a "drop in the bucket", so to speak.

This is not intended to be the complete history of the dams. It is a commentary to read after you have looked at the photographs. Most of the information comes from the files of the Josephine County Historical Society. We have files of photographs, newspaper clippings, articles written by various people for various reasons and filed with the Historical Society. I picked commentaries and photos which I thought would give insight into the existence of the dams. There are probably thousands of photos tucked away in old family albums and long established businesses that will never be seen and eventually discarded when the owner passes on or the business remodels, moves or closes. We urge you to share those photos with your local historical society.   Three photos of the Ament Dam ruins taken by teenagers in 1946 were delivered to the Historical Society in the spring of 2009.   They show how the silt has been deposited around the site over the years. If you have old photos, not just of the dams, but anything significant to Josephine County, you can bring them in to our research library. If you have photos but do not wish to donate them to the Society, we can scan them while you wait, and give back your originals.

The photos in this book start at Gold Ray Dam and come downstream. This commentary starts at Grants Pass and goes upstream. The Grants Pass Dam was a low diversion dam located just downriver from where Caveman Bridge is located today.   It was built to feed water into a power plant. There is very little written about the Grants Pass Dam, the Grants Pass Power Dam or the Grants Pass Diversion Dam, the many names it was called.   Details about the power plant are limited. The dam seemed to change names with each commentary. The *Rogue River Courier* had this short article on Oct. 22, 1903, and it only mentions the power plant because of what happened upstream. *"The closing of the Condor dam at Gold Ray Friday created a sensation in Grants Pass when the report that "Rogue River had gone dry" were circulated Saturday morning, and many of the residents went to the river to satisfy their curiosity. The water did fall to such an extent that the river resembled a brook. The Water, Light and Power Company's race was dry and numerous salmon were flopping in the mud. Friday night the water was too low to run the wheel and the city was in darkness."* As you read on, you find a similar incident attributed to the Golden Drift Dam. The Gold Ray incident is a documented event from a newspaper article. The Golden Drift incident was a hearsay comment passed to the present time by word of mouth.

If you want to see something that still exists from that time, walk across the down stream side of Caveman Bridge and look down at the river. You will see the remains of the bridge supports of the previous bridge which was removed when Caveman Bridge opened in 1931. Look down stream and compare what you see with the pictures in this book.

One post card at the Josephine County Historical Society calls the Grants Pass Dam the Caveman Dam. It was built before 1895 because the following short article gives us a reference date. The article is dated March 30, 1895 but gives no source. *"The Gold Beach Gazette is still harping about the dam across Rogue River at Grants Pass and claims that the obstructions in the river here in the way of fish traps and dams are ruining fishing interests of Rogue River."* In January of 1923 the flood washed out a large potion of the dam. It was repaired many times. It was continually fixed as floods took out portions of the dam. These two short articles, eight years apart, mention the recreational value of the dam. In August 1926 it was noted, *"Better success than had been anticipated is reported on the work of repairing the old dam below the Sixth Street bridge. With the work only about half done, the water has been raised about six inches at the bath house, and H. A. Corlee (Corless?), who is doing the work, declares that when he is through the water will be at least a foot higher."*

An article of June 23, 1934 states: *"Inspection of the old rock-crib dam over Rogue River just below the Sixth Street bridge by city officials revealed that the dam had virtually disintegrated, presents but a slight barrier to water on the south side of the river. Held together by willow trees and brush that had grown up through the remains of the cribbing. Alternate proposal of moving the bathhouse up stream in "The Oaks" or rebuilding the present dam to raise the water level and fill the rock bottom with sand is being considered."*

In the end, when the dam was no longer holding back the lake, young willow trees took root in the wood and the mud the dam held. Prior to the 1964 flood, the location of the dam was more apparent. The riffle just past the Caveman Bridge is the site of the location of the dam. It went diagonally across the river angling northwest. If you look carefully at the photos, then go stand on Caveman Bridge, you can almost imagine it still exists. If you are in your sixties, or seventies, or eighties, you can remember the dam and the swimming hole at Riverside Park in various stages of decline.

The Grants Pass Dam created a small lake that was used for recreation with sail boats, canoes, covered boats and, of course, swimming with the bathhouse available to change clothes. There was a marina where people could rent boats to use on the lake. The bandstand/bathhouse on the south side of the river at Riverside Park was built because the lake was a popular swimming area. One commentary mentioned that originally the dam only raised the water about five feet, more than enough to make the area by the park a great swimming hole. In later years, the height of the water was lower. There was even a giant slide for swimmers to "swoosh" into the water. There are a few pictures of such activities. However, as you probably noticed, the lake looked much larger in 1911 than the river looks in 2009. As mentioned above, in 1926 they were trying to get it just a foot deeper. As you go downstream, past the bridge, there are old pieces of cement along the north shore that probably were the foundation of the ditch or powerhouse.

The next dam upstream about three miles from Grants Pass was the Ament Dam, built in 1902-1904 as part of the operations of the Golden Drift Mining Company. The initial low dam was called the Golden Drift Dam and was only slightly higher than the Grants Pass Dam. When it was raised higher to hold more water, it became the Ament Dam. It was built by C. W. Ament and his son Marion. The powerhouse was built so they could provide electricity to operate the Golden Drift Mine and they eventually planned to install bigger electric generators and sell the excess electricity. They had grand plans and eventually built a giant structure, the largest of the five dams. One bit of hearsay, which may have been an indication of management of the system in the future was that in 1903 when the initial filling of the dam began, they cut off the flow of the river, instead of letting it rise gradually and keeping the river flowing. This caused the Rogue River to almost go dry below the dam. Local miners ran to the river's midpoint and gathered as much muck as they could from beneath the exposed riverbed rocks and, as the story goes, found a considerable amount of gold flakes before the mistake was rectified and the flow of the river restored. Since a newspaper article said the same thing at the same time at Gold Ray Dam, also known as Condor Dam, the story about Golden Drift is probably in error since it is highly unlikely similar events would happen at the same time. The probable explanation is that the restriction of the flow at Condor also caused Golden Drift to lack water to flow over the spillway.

Records indicate they planned to make Ament Dam a source of electricity after the mining project became exhausted in two or three decades, but it did not go as originally intended as economics, the need for irrigation, floods and the survival of the fish kept the dam in continual change. The planned irrigation canals to take water into the city of Grants Pass were started and some completed but others never finished. Ament Dam had an interesting existence but it was operational for less than 20 years. Part of the powerhouse, which was never operated to its capacity, is still standing, although over half of it is buried in the sand at the up-river end of Tom Pearce Park

Following is an article from the *Oregon Observer,* June 14, 1902. This was photocopied from a copy of the original newspaper and increased in size for easy reading. Hereafter, segments from the newspaper have been edited and retyped. I did not go through every available newspaper so this is not a complete commentary of the dams as reported in the newspapers.

The Dry Diggings Dam.

Work is Being Pushed With all Speed,—Many men at Work.—Ditch Survey.

A representative of the OBSERVER made a visit to the Dry Diggings last Saturday and was kindly shown by M. C. Ament, manager, what is being done and what remains to be done by the Golden Drift Mining Company. Some 35 or 40 men are at work at present and a larger crew will be employed later on in order to get the dam in before the freshets of the winter season arrive. Mr. Ament says that they have been making very good progress, their only delays being occasioned by their unability to get material and machinery. So many things that they had to have were not to be had on the coast and sending East for them caused much delay and annoyance.

They have had their sawmill in operation for some time past and have over 350,000 feet of timber sawed which is nearly enough for the construction of the dam. They are cutting their timber from their own ground, sawing 12 x12 pieces for the construction of the cribs. Only first class lumber is used. Each piece must be free from knots, and perfectly clear in every particular. Their mill is operated by a 45 horse power gasoline engine. The whole is a marvel of modern-day mechanics, while the engine, mill and all can be loaded almost in entirely on a truck wagon, it saws regularly from 8,000 to 10,000 feet daily.

A number of cabins, mess and bunk houses, and other buildings are being constructed at the dam. A good road has been built leading from the main highway down to the river. The company has acquired all of the land from the rives back to the mountains east, and a considerable tract on the opposite side,—over 1000 acres in all.

As mentioned previously in the OB-SERVER, a better site for a dam than that selected by the Golden Drift company could not have been chosen. At this point the river narrows down to a width of 235 feet with a sheer bank of 35 feet on the west side and a 25 foot receding cement bank on the other, this being a veritable shelf rock which slopes back to the nearby mountains. On the shelf rock the power houses will be built. About one-half of the wing dam has already been constructed across this. This part of the dam is being built simply to protect the power houses in case of exceptionally high water.

The main cribs for the dam will be 100 feet wide on the bottom of the river and 80 feet wide across the top. The dam will be set 55 feet into the east bank in order to withstand the cutting power of the Rogue at high water. Even at an ordinary stage the river has a flow of 100 feet per second at this point.

On Saturday a large cable was drawn across the river and securely anchored, for the scow that is being built and will be launched later. This scow together with a gasoline engine drum and cable, and derrick will do the heavy work of carrying out and setting the crib timbers in place. One man by the touch of a lever will be able to do more than several hundred men could in twice the time. Two powerful gasoline engines have been set in place at the dam for the manipulation of the derricks and cables.

The dam will be nearly 500 feet in length over all, with a 300 foot opening on the river. The race will be 90 feet in width and will be cut through the cement bank on the west shore. Six turbines capable of furnishing 3000-horse power will be installed. These wheels will furnish power for the battery of pumps that will force the water up the pipe line to the diggings where six giants will be kept thundering against the auriferous gravel banks every day and every night the entire year through; and there is ground enough to keep the giants going for a hundred years to come.

Aside from the pumps that will operate the giants a separate system of rotary pumps will be installed to supply the two irrigating ditches that are to be put in. There will be two of these, one on each side of the Rogue. The survey for the east side ditch has already been completed and the surveyors are now at work surveying the one for the west side. These ditches will be flowing water for next season's crops. They will reach and irrigate all of the farms and orchards between Grants Pass and the dam, as well as farms and orchards for several miles below the city. All parts of Grants Pass will be reached by the east side ditch, which as stated has already been surveyed.

These ditches will make a garden of Eden of this section of the Rogue river valley. There are but few things that will not grow in the fertile Josephine county soil when it can have water during the summer season.

The completion of the Rogue river dam will settle the question of future power for factories and all manufacturing purposes for all time in Grants Pass.

A five stage centrifugal pump, the largest ever manufactured up to 1904 by the Byron-Jackson Iron Works of San Francisco was installed at the dam site.   The pump, powered by five turbine water wheels delivering 1600 horse power to the pump shaft had an aggregated capacity of 10,000 gallons per minute under a 500 foot head. The operation of pumping water into some of the completed irrigation canals was successful for about 6 years.

About 1910 it was decided to convert the crib dam to a concrete structure. This work was well underway in 1912 when a major storm occurred, washing out the section where the old and new structures joined. The pump and turbine water wheels were lost to the Rogue River and it was impossible to recover and salvage any of the items.

The operation of Ament Dam went through upheaval and the final dream was never completed, although the dam served the community until 1921.   If you play Frisbee (disk) golf at Tom Pearce Park, you have probably seen the remains of the dam. If not, take a walk and see the grafitti covered structure with "1911" preserved in concrete. Go to the park, turn left at the first parking lot after you enter. Drive to the restroom building, park and follow the path upstream for about a quarter mile and see the century old ruins. The concrete structure is 200 feet above the river edge.   The remains of the dam might be more appreciated if one knows more of the story.   The following edited details were published in local newspapers. Notice changes from previous pages.

The October 17, 1903 *Oregon Observer* had an article about the building of the Golden Drift Dam. These are some of the details given in that issue of the paper:

"The power dam for the operation of the Golden Drift Mining Company, across the Rogue River at the Dry Diggings is about completed.   The structure is built up to its required height across the river, and workmen are now filling in the cribs. This work is being done by a steam shovel and cars, there being a half dozen of the later pulled by a cable and kept running to and from the steam shovel out over the dam.

"The main structure, or the dam itself, will be completed before the winter rains set in.   The machinery will not be put in till next spring. The dam will be capable of supplying 10,000 horsepower to begin with, much of which will be used for operating the monster pumps that will supply the giants in the Dry Digging placer with water. The Golden Drift Company owns nearly 1000 acres of placer ground in the Dry Diggings that will be piped off when the dam is completed and the pumps and giants installed. This ground will be sufficient in area to keep a battery of four or five giants busy for the next 25 or 35 years."   (In 1902 article it was 100 years of mining; a year later only 25 or 35.)

In 1903 they had high hopes for the Golden Drift Mining Company. It was never fully realized but the story is still fascinating, although rather obscure to most residents of Grants Pass. The preceding paragraph may seem odd to someone who does not know the terms mentioned. What is placer mining? What is a giant? Here is a look into our past that most individuals do not remember and may not be aware of because timber was the product we grew up knowing. Mining and agriculture were the main occupations that built Josephine County. Many of us lament the loss of timber jobs but timber, logging, lumber mills, etc. fill only a brief part of the history of Josephine County. Prior to 1950, mining was one of the primary occupations of the local population. The timber industry started to be developed after World War II. Prior to that it was mining and gold was the primary quest, although Josephine County produced well in chrome, cement, bauxite and minor minerals. There were also minor pockets of jewels such a rubies and garnets, but no mention of diamonds. The Aments wanted to catch and save anything of value that washed out of Dry Diggings.

Who were the Aments and where did they come from? The following biographies of the Aments were in the Historical Society files, but no date or source was attached. The articles, by today's standards, seem to glorify the Ament family. Knowing the source and author might shed some light on the situation and clarify the intentions of the articles.

C.G. Ament, president of the Golden Drift Mining Company was born November 5, 1851, at the old homestead in Kendall county, Ill. His occupation has been varied, from reclaiming large tracts of arid lands, to developing the virgin prairies into high priced productive farmlands. He was educated in high schools and institutes of learning, and is a gentleman of retiring manner and is a worthy citizen of high moral character and Christian integrity. His marriage united him with Miss Emma Simms, a highly cultured lady, and they are blessed with three children, two of whom are boys.

Mr. Ament is a firm believer in irrigation, and was instrumental in obtaining signatures to the project which was to convert many thousand acres of otherwise worthless land into rich, productive farms which today are teeming in wealth in fat growing kine. He left his rich pastures and beautiful meadows in Colorado, all under a double water right, to superintend the irrigating proposition of the beautiful and productive valley of Grants Pass, Ore., of which he is the leading factor. The Aments are all hustlers and have a happy faculty of succeeding.

C.W. Ament, the general manager of the Golden Drift Mining Company, is a brother of C.G.Ament, whose father, E.G. Ament, now deceased, came to Chicago in 1824, when there were but three houses in the town. This was before the Indian War of the white settlers with the Sacs, Foxes and the Black Hawks and in the days when the plow was drawn by the faithful ox-team, in the perilous period when the trusty rifle was always a factor of the plowman's safety as the swish of an Indian's arrow or the flash of an old flint lock from ambush was not an uncommon occurrence. It was during these early days that Shabbona, the old Indian chief, advised all of the white families of the Fox River Valley of the pending massacre by the coming redskin warriors; a fact which made old Shabbona's name revered and was ever after a shibboleth of good cheer and great reverence. Shabbona often camped by the "old spring" at the Ament home, always being the modest recipient of fat mince and apple pies from the hot bake-oven of the ever faithful wife and mother Ament, as well as a heaping milkpan of doughnuts done to a brown.

C.W. Ament was born in Kendall County, Ill., September 17, 1842, and started on the road of life by taking up the common school branches in an old log school house situated on the farm; after which he attended high school at Plainfield and later attended Fowler Institute. He married Miss Lucy J. Preston by whom two children were born, Marion C. and Winifred L. Ament, both of whom are living. Later in life he became a large rancher in New Mexico and finally took up mining, and after years of experience he decided to purchase a placer property with a great future, if such could be found, and finally selected the Dry Diggings. Having conceived the idea of installing large hydraulic pumps for mining purposes after a most careful investigation of all possibilities, he decided to construct a dam across Rogue River, which he regards as the crowing effort of his life.

M.C. Ament, superintendent of the Golden Drift Mining Company, was born in Livingston county, Ill., in 1869 and is the eldest child of C.W. and Lucy J. (Preston) Ament. His childhood days were spent near Chicago, Ill. and in Topeka, Kans., and his education was obtained principally in Washburn College and the Topeka Business College. He married Miss Edith Cavell, an English lady, by whom he has two children. A close application for years in the Santa Fe shops and many other mechanical and electrical undertakings gave him his broad initiation into the occupation of which he is now an acknowledged expert.

In politics Mr. Ament has always been a pronounced Republican, but not a partisan nor an office seeker, preferring to devote himself wholly to his business interests. Since coming to Grants Pass in December, 1901, he has been a member of the board of trade and is identified with other organizations for the upbuilding of the place.

As superintendent of the construction of the Golden Drift Dam, Mr. Ament has had abundant opportunity to utilize his inventive and mechanical genius. This gigantic dam, which is seven hundred feet over all, is twenty and one-half feet high and one hundred and twenty feet wide at the bottom, with a converging thirty-degreed slope, to fourteen feet wide at the top of the dam. The other dimensions are as follows: Four hundred feet across the river; an eighty-foot abutment; a raceway one hundred and twenty feet in width; and a wing dam three hundred and fifty feet in length (the latter being for the purpose of protecting the power house). The total possible power output is forty-one thousand horse-power, of which six thousand horse-power will be used for hydraulicing at the mines and the balance for irrigation and for sale to outlying industries. In the near future, large electric generators will be put in and other improvement made for transmission purposes.

The company owns eleven hundred acres of auriferous or gold bearing gravel, forming one of the largest and richest placers in the entire state of Oregon, the banks running from twenty to ninety feet in depth. The plant will be ready for operation by 1904, and will then be operated night and day, power being thereby secured sufficient for the removal of six thousand yards of gravel per day. Under the supervision of M. C. Ament, sawmills were installed for the company and a sufficient amount of lumber (about two million, five hundred thousand feet) sawed for the completion of the plant. The steam shovel used for excavating the raceway was built under his personal supervision and its signal success voices the wisdom of this undertaking. Mr. Ament's ability along mechanical lines has been of great assistance to him in the trying duties assigned him, and his services as a skilled mechanic have been the greatest value of the company and have enabled its directors (of whom he is one) to place the plant upon a solid financial and practical working basis. This enterprise will prove a giant stride in the mining world that will prove the true value of force with which to uncover the upper granite bedrock and disclose the vast age-hidden treasure of incalculable value in the silent mountain peaks.

Therefore when the Aments wanted to build a big dam to use the water for mining and offered the leftover water for irrigation and leftover power for public consumption, it sounded like a good plan. According to the previous articles, the Aments certainly had good credentials and obviously in 1904, being a "hustler" was a good thing.

Placer mining needs lots of water to operate the giants. Placer mining is the washing away of the alluvial top layers of the soil and allowing the heavier gold to settle to the bottom. There are several methods of retrieving the gold after it is "washed out." One of the most common was to run the slurry mix into sluice boxes, where the heavier gold, and sometimes gemstones, would settle to the bottom and the dirt and gravel washed away. To wash it out of the alluvial soil, giant nozzles are aimed at the site and it is eroded away by the water. In mountain placer mining, ditches and flumes were built to funnel the water into the giants by gravity flow. Most mountain mining operations took place in the winter when the rain provided sufficient water to keep the ditches flowing. Along rivers gravity flow could also work, but a mine could be worked year round with a supply of dammed water and electrical powered pumps to direct the water through the giants. Golden Drift Dam was the start and Ament Dam was the end. The Golden Drift Dam was not sufficient to survive the floods that occasionally come down the Rogue River, and in 1905 one of those floods hit the dam. The Golden Drift Mine Company sent out a letter to their stockholders, explaining the problem. A copy of that letter is on the following page.

Also following the letter is a old, fuzzy picture of the dam as taken from the hill to the north west of the dam. This shows the lower dam to the right with the lake behind it and what looks like the newer concrete portion to the left. The photo is so fuzzy, it was not included with the photos in the main section of this book. It was probably photographed about 1911.

Following the photo are two views of a professionally hand drawn map from the time of the expansion of the dam. The first shows an overall view and the second is just an enlargement showing the details a bit closer.

The final insertions in this section are two pages of small newspaper clippings found in an envelope in the "dams" file at the Josephine County Historical Society.

C. G. AMENT, President   M. C. AMENT, Secretary and Treasurer

The Golden Drift Mining Co. of Oregon

MINES AND POWER PLANT AT
GRANTS PASS, OREGON

REPOSITORY
   GRANTS PASS BANKING & TRUST CO.
CORRESPONDENT
   STATE BANK, CHICAGO, ILLINOIS

Grants Pass, Oregon,   Nov. 24, 1906

To the Stockholders of the Golden Drift Mining Co:

We herewith beg to submit a brief statement concerning the Golden Drift. Something like one year ago we were visited with an unfortunate flood which damaged the property some and delayed us for eight or ten months; it filled in our raceway below the dam by pushing around the wing dam, pouring over the bank and came well nigh undermining the great pump; this necessitated our building a substructure on bedrock and bring it up to the pump base which is now securely done and the pump is resting on a cement foundation.

Owing to high water which rolled four feet over the entire wheels, penstock, lineshafting, etc., and the consequent filling in of our race it was necessary to build a dredge which took nearly all summer as we dared not place it on the water till all danger from high water had subsided; this finished and the raceway cleared we set about building a great wall of piling and timbers something like 250 x 300 feet in area, this is now being filled in with rock to a depth of 30 feet to insure against a similar occurence; also a crib of heavy timbers is built at right angles with the dam and at point of overflow which is also to be filled with rock 10 feet high to shunt the high water around the plant, to bring about this great undertaking has cost lots of patient thought, anxiety, time and money. We are now building a 500 flume together with up to date saving tables, twenty-two or more in number where we had barely one before, to save the fine gold and black sand much of which has been lost heretofore. We have not completed this as yet, having only twelve tables in and this discloses the fact that we have Garnets and Rubies among the black sand, all of which adds to the values to be saved.

We hope to give a more detailed statement a little later embodying the results of our departure in new gold saving devices which must of necessity be a great improvement over the old method.

Yours truly,

GOLDEN DRIFT MINING CO.

  This photo was taken before the dam was enlarged but the rectangular "building" to the left of the river, looks like the part that is still standing at Tom Pearce Park. If it is the concrete structure, then this photo was taken c. 1911.

omme, Portland, Or.

4   3   2   1

Jones Cr.

East Fork

9   10   11   12

Bloody Run

Hill

Hill.

Acre Tracts #100 to #400 per Acre

Elevation 100 to 250 feet.

City Limits

Smith

Granite

Colvig 40 A.

Day. 40 A.

15

Golden Nugget

Drift Min. Co. Lodes

14   13

Sherman Land.

McElmer 63 Acres.

Dimon 40 A.

Perry 40 A.

Golden

Drift Min. Co.

Proposed Ditch Line 130 feet Elevation.

40 A.

55 A.

Fine

Dimon 40 A.

Drift Min. Co.

Power Dam.

Fruit Lands

Sharp Bros.

Jo. Moss

Golden

Pete Golden

B. R. T.

51 Acres.

Haviland

Cantew

Ray

Ray

23   24

22

Ray Ray

Ray.

Old Orch. Farm 117 A. Thoma

Adams Rail Road.

Prof. Tunnen Ray Ray of High School.

Bald Mountain

Lands here held at $25. to $50. per acre

28   27   26   25

Ray

Knob.

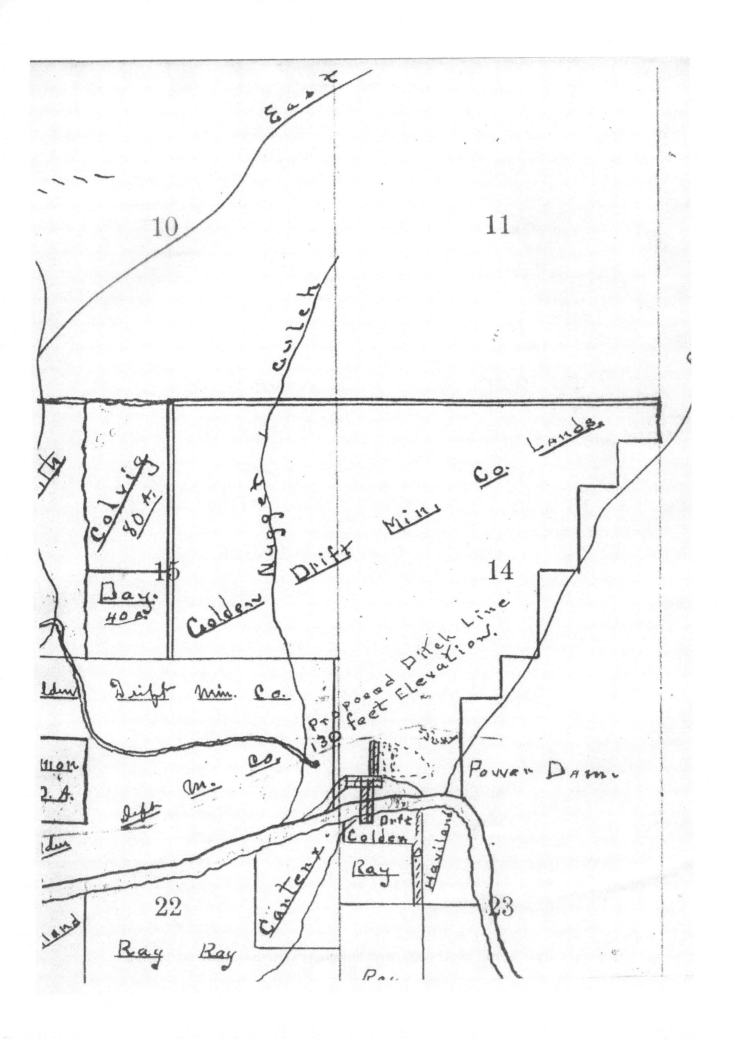

The Gold Beach Gazette is still harping about the dam across Rogue river at Grants Pass and claims that the obstructions in the river here in the way of fish traps and dams are ruining fishing interests of Rogue river. (The dam referred to is the one just below t h e Sixth street bridge that furnished power for the electric light plant.) 3-30-1895

From the Rogue River Courier
October 22, 1903
The closing of the Condor dam at Gold Ray Friday created a sensation in Grants Pass when the report that "Rogue river had gone dry" were circulated Saturday morning, and many of the residents went to the river to satisfy their curiosity. The water did fall to such an extent that the river resembled a brook. The Water, Light and Power company's race was dry and numerous salmon were flopping in the mud. Friday night the water was too low to run the wheel and the city was in darkness.

8-7-26

Better success than had been anticiapted is reported on the work of repairing the old dam below the Sixth street bridge. With the work only aobut half done, the water has been raised about six inches at the bath house, and H. A. Corless, who is doing the work, declares that when he is through the water will be at least a foot higher.

In 1926 8/6

Better success than had been anticipated is reported on the work of repairing the old dam below the Sixth Street bridge.
With the work only about half done, the water has been raised about six inches at the bath house, and H.A. Corlee, who is doing the work, declares that when he is through the water will be at least a foot higher.

6/23/3f

Inspection of the old r o c k-crib dam over Rogue river just below the Sixth-street bridge by city officials revealed that the dam had virtually disintegrated, presenting but a slight barrier to water on the south side of the river. Held together by willow trees and brush that had grown up through the remains

of the cribbing. Alternate proposal of moving the bathhouse up stream to "The Oaks" or rebuilding the present dam to raise the water level and fill the rock bottom with sand is being considered.

These clippings, with some duplicates, talk about various dams in our region.

The Gold Beach Gazette is still harping about the dam across Rogue river at Grants Pass and claims that the obstructions in the river here in the way of fish traps and dams are ruining fishing interests of Rogue river. (The dam referred to is the one just below the Sixth street bridge that furnished power for the electric light plant.) 3-30-1895

Wimer Bros. are putting in a new dam in the Illinois river, their old dam having washed out last winter. They are getting their mine nicely opened up. 9-12-1896

Messrs. Taylor and Savage have started to wing dam Rogue river just above Savage rapids, where there is a rich bar. 6-10-1897

From the Rogue River Courier
October 22, 1903
The closing of the Condor dam at Gold Ray Friday created a sensation in Grants Pass when the report that "Rogue river had gone dry" were circulated Saturday morning, and many of the residents went to the river to satisfy their curiosity. The water did fall to such an extent that the river resembled a brook. The Water, Light and Power company's race was dry and numerous salmon were flopping in the mud. Friday night the water was too low to run the wheel and the city was in darkness.

3-31-05
Salmon are now plentiful in the Applegate and its tributaries. It has been a long time since salmon have been this far up the streams. The fish ladder constructed at the irrigation dam at Wilderville seems to have failed in its purpose as the fish seemed unable to pass up it. Now that the dam has been washed out there are plenty of fish in the upper Applegate.

In 1905 6/13
Considerable trouble is being experienced by the Murphy Irrigation company to hold their dam in the Applegate. The dam is constructed with sacks of sand. The eels work holes in the sacks and water washes the sand out of the sacks, then sand and sacks go down the river.

On Oct. 27 in 1906
Construction officials plan to build a long dam across Bear Creek at a point where it narrows north of Ashland. The project will create a storage lake of 1,000 acres in extent.

From the Daily Courier
Week Ending July 30, 1920
First construction started Saturday on the 500-foot concrete diversion dam at Savage Rapids dam for the big gravity project of the Grants Pass Irrigation district. Work will now be prosecuted under the highest pressure, with day and night crews working the equipment on hand 24 hours in the day in order to accomplish the necessary construction during the low stage of the river.

1-21-21
The recent high water of the Rogue has taken out a portion of the concrete work on the old Golden Drift dam above town, the portion destroyed being between the spillway and the north side. Water is now running through the break and the crest of the spillway is reported to be several feet above the high water mark.

Two workmen at the Golden Drift dam made some extra money Friday night when they dragged the river at the dam to recover fishing tackle and line. Their total haul was 34 spoons, many sinkers, and about 2000 feet of fine fishing line in lengths from 100 to 300 feet.
5-20-21

— 9-16-21
The coffer dam, shutting off all water from the by-pass at the Savage Rapids dam, has been completed. The entire flow of the river is now being sent through the four sluice gates under the power house, these gates being 4x6 feet each.

In 1926 8/6
Better success than had been anticipated is reported on the work of repairing the old dam below the Sixth Street bridge.
With the work only about half done, the water has been raised about six inches at the bath house, and H.A. Corlee, who is doing the work, declares that when he is through the water will be at least a foot higher.

From the Daily Courier
Week Ending December 31, 1934
A temporary organization for the purpose of furthering a proposal to build a 100-foot dam on Applegate river at the Barr ranch was definitely formed Wednesday night at the Applegate community hall. The new group will be known as the Applegate River Irrigation and Improvement district.

With preliminary excavations well under way, heavy construction on Shasta dam, major unit of the huge $170,000,00 central valley project, is slated to start Oct. 22 following ceremonies at which Interior Secretary Harold Ickles will speak. speak. 10-15-38

4-9- In 1936
Wednesday morning, workmen blocked the gates of the Savage Rapids irrigation dam, marking the official opening of the Grants Pass district's irrigation season, if not the actual summer weather.

The following is information from the April 23rd, 1909 *Rogue River Courier*.

The great Ament Dam across the Rogue River is to furnish water for the irrigation ditches of Josephine County and has a history which dates back to 1902. The dam is a substantial structure made in crib form from 12 by 12 sawed timber. The base of the dam is 125 feet in width and 27 ½ feet high with a perpendicular drop of 20 feet. A substantial bulkhead 30 feet in height, and 80 feet in width and 120 feet in length, resting upon the river bank and bedrock cement all filled with heavy boulders and cement gravel and planked over with double 3 inch planks and spiked with 12 inch spikes. The raceway is cut just beyond the bulkhead in the mainland with a head race 18 feet in depth and the tail race 30 feet in depth and 120 feet in width. The powerhouse site is situated beyond the raceway on the riverbank 200 feet from the river on bedrock. The entire structure including the wing dam is 720 feet overall requiring 3,500,000 feet of sawed timber to build at a cost of nearly a third of a million dollars excusive of the thousand acres of placer mining land adjoining the property.

The raceway gates are 12 in number, each 10 feet in width. The pen stock is furnished for 16-400 h.p. turbines giving 6400 h.p. When completed, it will have a capacity of 9600 h.p. Four wheels are installed and attached to steel gears. All coupled up and harnessed up to a 70 foot line shaft running in Phosphor Brown's ring oiling boxers and attached to a mammoth five step high lift centrifugal pump weighing 88,000 pounds, that has a capacity of 9,000 gallons per minute or 13,000,000 gallons per day when operating under a 430 foot head. It is the largest high lift centrifugal pump in the world. This pump is connected with a 22 inch steel discharge pipe 1500 feet in length with a full equipment of high pressure cut-off gates and monitors terminating at the point of diversion and is capable of delivering a 22 inch steam of water to an elevation 450 feet continuously from the power derived from 4,400 h.p. water wheels installed in tandem. This dam was built and equipped with power for placer mining and irrigation purposes. During the month of February, 1909, a contract was entered into with the owners of the great dam by the Josephine County Irrigation and Power Company for a supply of water for their ditches. The gravity ditches to be supplied direct from the dam and the water from the highline canals to be supplied by the great centrifugal pump. The utilization of this dam and power made it possible to supply water for irrigation during the present season. The irrigation company has an option on the dam which will run until 1911 at which time it is expected that the entire property will be taken over by the irrigation company.

The next major article located in a local newspaper is from the October 15, 1913 *Oregon Observer*.

In 1909, dissatisfied stockholders of the Golden Drift Mining Company operating about three miles east of Grants Pass, delegated George E. Sanders to investigate the affairs of the company, with power to enter suit if deemed necessary, against C.W. Ament, President of the company, and a resident of Grants Pass. The result was that the suit was entered in the circuit court here by the Golden Drift Mining Company against C.W. Ament. A great deal of evidence was taken and great interest was manifested in this neighborhood. The court deferred judgement, and it was not until last week that a decision was rendered by Judge Calkins, who found for the Golden Drift Company, and required Ament to account for moneys received in behalf of the mining company. This is the beginning of the end of this *important suit, which may be carried to the State Supreme Court for final judication. It is a matter that considerably concerns Grants Pass and vicinity. In the meantime a majority of the Chicago stockholders, finding that there was no mine to operate, organized a new company, the Chicago Rogue River Company for irrigation purposes and took possession of what is commonly known as the Ament Dam three miles up the Rogue River and which at that time has suffered severely from high water. Mr. Sanders was put in charge and vigorously pushed the needed repair, and put the dam in better condition then it had been theretofore. But the business was a failure. The Chicago Rogue River Company went into bankruptcy with a considerable amount of aggregate liabilities to merchants of this city, who furnished supplies. The capital of the Golden Drift Company was $1,500,000. This dam greatly concerns Grants Pass and vicinity. It is capable of supplying an extensive irrigation system and could be used for electric light and power. The final issue will be eagerly looked for, though it is likely to be long delayed.*

Time passed and water filled the irrigation ditches some of the time. Then it literally blew up. The following commentary comes from the July 16, 1916 *Rogue River Courier:*

Through the action of vandals who last night dynamited the big driving pulley that operated the pumps for the south side ditches at Golden Drift Dam, the farmers on the South side of the river and in the Fruitdale district will be without water for the balance of the season. (Evidently, since Ament had lost control of the dam, some reverted to calling it by its original name, ie. Golden Drift Dam.) The damage occurred at about 12:30 last night just after the water had been turned upon the turbines by Ike Davis, who was in charge. The vandals apparently slipped in between the exiting of Mr. Cargill, the night watchman, and the entry of Davis. The force of the explosion broke the heavy pulley, 6 feet in diameter, and the 48 inch face into bits and the 41 inch leather belt that connected it with the pump was torn and broken into pieces. This belt alone cost $1500 and to replace it and the pulley will take weeks of time. The pulley was worth about $350. and the other damage will run the loss to $2500. Mr. Davis said he saw no smoke from burning fuses when he entered the pump room. Powder burns on the pulley shaft shows that the charge must have been fastened at that point. Mr. Davis was behind a 10 inch column when the explosion occurred and did not get hit by any of the broken pulley. The force of the explosion hurling chunks of iron about was stong enough to rip holes in the heavy fir planking of the roof. The suspicion falls on any one or number of ditch workers or dam workers that have not been paid by the Public Service Corp. with Mr. George Sanders as president. At a meeting last night it was thought that those matters had been addressed to the satisfaction of all. Since the troubles over the payment of wages between the Public Service Corp. and the ditch workers and dam laborers, there have been numerous threats of personal violence against the officers of the company and occasionally it was stated by the laborers that no water should go into the ditches until they had been paid. The claimants have arranged through their attorneys, that payment would be made at specific dates in the future. At a meeting of the water users also last night, Mr. Sanders had agreed to put the pump all in good order and turn them over to the water users during the present season. A thorough investigation is to be made and the guilty party or parties will be brought to justice.

Five days later, this information was in the *Rogue River Courier*, July 30, 1916:

Some of the partys that have investigated the wreck of the big pulley and belt that operated the pumps for the Fruitdale ditch at the Golden Drift Mining Company Dam advance the opinion that the pulley may have burst in starting it up at an excessive speed. If this should prove true, it would disprove the dynamite theory that has been generally been given as responsible for the accident. Mr. Davis contends that the machinery had not yet gained speed, the explosion occurred when the big six foot pulley had made only two or three revolutions. Machinists have made a thorough examination of the damage and believe that it might be possible to have the pump repaired in time to again have water turned into the Fruitdale ditch before the end of the week. There is an old pulley that was formerly used, now available and while not as satisfactory as the one that was wrecked it would probably fill the bill. A belt is available at Portland and if the finances can be arranged by the water users it is likely that the belt will be ordered down today. It is possible that by getting a belt the pump could be put into operation by Thursday. Governor Withycombe wired district attorney Miller Saturday morning to the effect that there are no funds available for the offering of a reward for the apprehension of parties who may have been responsible for the wrecking of the pumps. County judge Gillette, however has stated that he believes the county could post a reward of $500; if the citizens so desired. No action has been taken.

It seems that then, as now, jumping to conclusions can make the proverbial mountain out of a mole hill. The August 2, 1916 *Rogue River Courier* had the following short article: " *Structure weakness was found to be the cause of the big pulley's demise at the Golden Drift Dam. After a grand jury hearing and listening to other witnesses, Judge Calkins of Medford decided there was no foul play.*"

The dynamite theory was discounted. However, another problem with the dam which had existed since the day it started to hold back the flow of the river, finally came to the forefront. Environmentalists, although not called by that name in 1916, had long lamented about the fish runs. They believed that the existence of the dam, with the poor fish ladders, was causing the fish to fail to reach the upstream spawning grounds in sufficient numbers to keep the Rogue River well supplied with an annual crop of fish.
Fish from the Rogue River were not just there for the once-in-awhile sportsman in 1916 the mid-point of the War to End All Wars. World War I was being fought in Europe and food was rationed in the United States. Some local citizens even appealed to the Federal food administrator, recounting the dying fish at the base of the dam, unable to swim upstream. As one might recall, the food administrator was Herbert Hoover, born in Iowa but raised in Oregon, later to become President of the United States. What Hoover did, if anything, is not noted in our files at the Josephine County Historical Society. What the local Oregon state game warden did, probably thinking Hoover might approve, is recorded in the March 8, 1918 *Courier*:

State game warden Carl D. Shoemaker acting under instructions from the state fish and game commission, Sunday blasted an "adequate fishway" at the Ament Dam by dynamiting the coffer dam running from the concrete portion of the dam back to the North shore, thus enabling fish to ascend by the ladder as well as through the gap torn through the coffer dam. The effect was immediately apparent, the imprisoned fish below began to ascent at once.

Before the commission acted, the bureau of hatcheries had appealed to the food administrator to authorize the dam as a menace to the food supply, presenting figures showing that the fish were prevented from reaching the spawning beds and hatchery work curtailed. The state food administrator referred the matter to Mr. Hoover with a favorable report, but the delay caused by investigation would have stopped the spring run of salmon even if finally acted upon.

About a month later, the game warden's appearance in court was reported in the April 5, 1918 *Courier:*

Carl D .Shoemaker, State game warden who was in Southern Oregon on business, was called to appear in Federal Court Monday before Judge Woolveton to show cause why he should not be considered in contempt of court for blowing up the Ament Dam several weeks ago. On Sunday, March 3rd the state game warden, accompanied by Deputy game warden Walker, Jack Altpent and others secured a powder man from Grants Pass and blew up the coffer dam with dynamite. The receiver for the Rogue River Public Service Corporation filed a complaint against this action, and Mr. Shoemaker's arrest was the result. Mr. Shoemaker will base his defense on the ground that summary action was imperative to conserve the food supply in Southern Oregon during the war.

Since it had been known for years that Ament Dam had blocked the fish passage, and any person that fished the Rogue over the years could clearly see a decline, the case was dropped. A secondary reason for the dropping of the case was that approval had been granted for the removal of all fish hindering obstacles, but it had not arrived at the time of the dynamiting. A third and less mentioned reason was the war and regulation of a good and stable food supply.

However, since there was no legal action, to keep the flow open, the dam was repaired and more successful fish ladders built. Mother Nature tried to do what the legal system was slow on acting upon, by providing higher water than the dam could handle in the winter of 1918-1919. Rumor had it that the dam had been taken out by the high water. The dam was only three miles upstream from downtown Grants Pass, but not many people visited the site.

According to a small newspaper clipping, a flood hit the dam site in January of 1923 taking out a large portion of the remaining portion of the dam. The same flood severely damaged the Grants Pass Diversion Dam. Ament Dam had not been functional since 1921 when part of it was dynamited in December about a month after the dedication of Savage Rapids Dam, two miles upstream. There were rumors that the attempts to remove Ament Dam earlier were somehow tied to the proposal to built Savage Rapids Dam just two miles upriver from Ament because the attempts to damage or destroy Ament happened after the decision to build Savage Rapids had been made.

Previously, when it looked like Ament Dam was destined for removal, a group of local citizens decided to apply to the State of Oregon for a water right to irrigate in and around Grants Pass. In about 1916, according to research done by Edna May Hill, some men from Salem came to the Grants Pass area to look at what might be done to provide a financially secure company to build and operate irrigation dams, with good fish ladders, of course. A Mr. Crawford and friends, looked at the river, and proposed that the best site to build a dam upstream from Grants Pass would be at Savage Rapids and another good site downstream would be at Hellgate. That company was formed as the Rogue River Irrigation and Power Company and they were able to get both sites for future dams. The Hellgate Dam (or whatever its final name would be) was destined to create a deep reservoir at Hellgate Canyon and provide irrigation water for the Merlin area. Savage Rapids Dam would have gravity flow ditches to provide for the Grants Pass area. The old ditches constructed to carry irrigation water from Ament Dam, would be used by the new dam. Eventually they merged with a local group and it became the Grants Pass Irrigation Company. The Savage Rapids site went ahead and contracts were awarded. Work at Savage Rapids began in 1920. The Hellgate portion passed into history and for the most part was forgotten. Savage Rapids was built with a power plant to contribute electricity to the grid and the gravity ditches into Grants Pass were completed, using some of the old Ament Dam ditches. The dam was dedicated in November 1921. In December of 1921, the old wooden portion of Ament Dam, two miles downstream from Savage Rapids, was dynamited to allow the fish to swim upstream. In 1923 a flood took out much of what remained of the wooden portion of Ament Dam. Savage Rapids was named after the Savage family and of course the dam was named after the rapids.

Savage Rapids Dam wasconstructed in 1920-21. It was finished and dedicated on Saturday, November 5, 1921. People who turn on a spigot to get water probably do not realize how long and complicated the process was to get water to our valley's crops. The convoluted history and difficult times during the existence of Ament Dam made people determined to build a dam for irrigation and only irrigation. The power house at Savage Rapids Dam was incidental to the main purpose of water for growing crops. In an article written for *The Oregon Observer* by C.K. Logan, November 9, 1921, Logan noted the need for water causing 3000 people to attend the dedication of the dam. This is part of his commentary: *"Sparkling in the sunshine of a perfect autumn day, the waters of the Rogue River were dedicated for irrigation purposes at the celebration for the completion of the Savage Rapids Dam and Grants Pass Irrigation District, where dreams of a quarter century became an actuality here Saturday.*

Lining both banks of the river, and extending far up the sides of the surrounding hills, a crowd estimated at 3000 witnessed the ceremonies marking the official opening of the project. People from nearby towns predominated, though many distinguished visitors were present for the occasion from many sections of the state and coast.

Speakers of the day made their addresses from a specially constructed platform about 100 yards below the south end of the dam, on account of the noise of the rushing water. Several pauses were necessitated by passing trains on the opposite side of the river, whistling to clear the right of way from those gathered there for the celebration."

The keynote speaker was Dr. W.J. Kerr, president of the Oregon Agricultural College (now Oregon State University) in Corvallis. After his speech, Althen Smith, the 15 year-old daughter of the president of the board of directors of the irrigation district, closed the switch at 3:15 PM. setting the machinery in motion. A powder charge was fired at the same moment the switch was closed. All was well and almost any crop suited for the climate could now be planted in the area knowing there was sufficient water for the crop to grow to maturity.

Savage Rapids Dam served the community from 1921 through 2008. Although Savage Rapids had what was considered sufficient fish ladders for 1921, and the fish seemed to be getting upstream, the jubilation did not last. Savage Rapids was continually upgraded to meet new and ever changing standards. After a major reconstruction in the 1950's, it seemed as if the problem may have been solved. About the time of the 200th birthday of the United States, more and more environmental groups were advocating the removal of dams throughout the nation. Savage Rapids Dam was one of the targeted dams. The question of irrigation was one of the major reasons it stood as long as it did The area the dam served is extremely dry. Some even said the leakage of the irrigation water flowing through the ditches in the region helped keep wells from going dry. Rainfall was insufficient for the needs of growing crops. Many wells might dry up if the water was not filling the ditches. Everybody had an opinion. The idea of removing the dam gained some favor when a plan of installing pumps to get the water out of the river and into the ditches was proposed.

To make a long story short, so to speak, it was finally decided to build the pumping station and then take out the dam. Removal of the dam began just before the 2009 irrigation season began. Glitches happened such as high water taking out part of the cofferdam just before removal began and then, later, low water caused the pumps to suck up sand and gravel and clog some of the pumps. Like Ament Dam, a portion of Savage Rapids will not be removed. It will remain as a reminder, to those who pay attention to local history, that dams along the Rogue River existed for a few decades and then mostly disappeared for the sake of the fish. Unlike Ament Dam, the Savage Rapids site will still take water from the river for irrigation. There is more than one pump, and we can only hope they will not all suffer breakdowns at the same time.

Above Savage Rapids, Gold Hill Dam was built in the early 1940s as a diversion dam to a power house and to provide water for the city of Gold Hill and the Ideal Cement Company. You can still see the power house if you turn left off of Hwy. 99 after crossing the south Gold Hill bridge and going under the railroad bridge. The large, deserted quarry of the Ideal Cement Company sits on the hill above Gold Hill. To see both the quarry and the dam site, exit the freeway at the north Gold Hill exit, the first exit as you go south from Grants Pass. Turn right on Hwy. 99 and cross the Rock Point bridge. Look to the left to see the old quarry and drive through the city of Gold Hill. To get to the dam site turn left off Hwy. 99 after you cross the second bridge and go about a mile after you drive under the railroad bridge and look across the river to the grey power house with most of the windows broken out. The dam was removed in the summer of 2008, but since it was off the main road, many people did not even know it was still there, in a rather deteriorated state, unless they happened to be unlucky enough to get their canoe or raft caught at the dam site. The dam was about 900 feet long and only 8 feet high. Every fish that went up or down the Rogue River had to pass over the dam. By 2010 it is hoped that the adjacent wetlands will be completely restored.

If you continue on the same road, you will come to Gold Ray Dam. It is a one-way narrow road and easy to travel until you meet someone coming downstream. If you see someone coming toward you, pull over at one of the narrow turnouts and let the downstream traffic pass. If you do not look far enough ahead to see oncoming vehicles, you may find that you will have to back up several hundred feet to let them pass. You might want to go back to Hwy. 99 and go to Tolo and turn left and take the paved road to Gold Ray Dam.

The first Gold Ray Dam was built in 1904 by two brothers, C.R. and Frank Ray. It was a wooden structure which raised the water high enough to pass through a power house and create the first hydro-electric power to the valley. A primitive fish ladder was built on the south side of the dam. In 1921 the dam became part of the California Oregon Power Company (Copco) which eventually became Pacific Power. In 1941 the old timber dam was removed and replaced with the present dam and a better fish ladder and a fish counter was added. By 1972, after almost seven decades of use, the rope-driven turbines had become difficult to keep up, almost obsolete, so they were retired and Gold Ray ceased to produce power.

With all five dams gone, the Rogue River will flow freely for 157 miles from Lost Creek Dam to the Pacific Ocean. Many see this as a wonderful event. Others have misgivings, but life goes on and the water will continue to flow.

Made in the USA
Middletown, DE
02 October 2020